Cinderella lived with two horrible sisters and
their mother.
They were very lazy and ugly too.
'Cinderella, bring me cake!'
'Cinderella, clean my bedroom!'
'Cinderella, bring me wool!' they said.

Poor Cinderella! From morning to night she
cleaned and cooked and washed.
She was very sad.
'Oh, this is terrible,' she said. 'All I do is
clean, clean, clean!'

One morning, at 10 o'clock, a letter arrived.

Come to the Ball!
The Castle
14th July at 8 o'clock
Beautiful clothes

WHERE?
WHEN?
DRESS?

'EXCELLENT!' said the ugly sisters. 'Let's go!'

Cinderella was very, very sad.
'I want to go to the ball too,' she said.
'But I have no dress or shoes to wear.'
She cried and cried.

Then – at 9 o'clock on the night of the ball:
Trrrrrrring!
'Wow! Who are you?' said Cinderella.
'I am your fairy godmother. I am here to help you,' said the lady.

Trrrrrring!
Cinderella had a beautiful dress and
shoes. 'Now – go to the ball!' said the fairy
godmother. 'But, at 12 o'clock, no later,
come home!'

When the prince saw Cinderella, he said,
'Wow! She's beautiful!'
'Would you like to dance with me?'
he asked her.

They danced all night.
The ugly sisters did not know it was Cinderella.
'Who is she?' they said.
'Who is that beautiful girl?'

Then Cinderella heard the clock.
'Oh, no, 12 o'clock,' she said.
'It's time to go!'
She ran quickly from the castle.
'Come back!' called the prince.
'Please don't go!'

But it was too late! It was after 12 o'clock!
Cinderella looked at her clothes and shoes.
'Oh no,' she said.
'Where are my beautiful dress and shoes!'
Poor Cinderella!

The prince was very sad.
'Oh, no, where is she?' he cried.
But... what is this?
'Ah, her beautiful little shoe,' he said.
'Now I will find her.'

The prince tried every foot in every house…
but it was no good! The shoe was too big or
too small.
'Where is she?' the prince said sadly.

Cinderella came from the kitchen.

Cinderella tried the shoe.
'YES! The shoe is YOURS,'
the prince said.
'YOU are the girl
I met at the ball.'

The prince asked Cinderella to marry him. She
said 'Yes!'
They soon got married and they were very,
very happy.
And the ugly sisters?
What do YOU think?

ACTIVITIES

BEFORE YOU READ

Look at the cover of the book.

1   Is Cinderella   **WHY?**

2   **Treasure Hunt.**
    Look at the pictures in the book. Can you find –

Cinderella   The ugly sisters   The shoe

The fairy   The beautiful dress   A letter

cakes   The prince   wool

AFTER YOU READ

1   Did you like the story –

2   Draw a picture of your favourite bit of the story.

WHY is it your favourite?

Pearson Education Limited
Edinburgh Gate, Harlow
Essex CM20 2JE, England
and Associated Companies throughout the world.

ISBN 0582 428688

First published by Librairie du Liban Publishers, 1996
This adaptation first published 2000 under licence by Penguin Books
© 2000 Penguin Books Limited
Illustrations © 1996 Librairie du Liban

1 3 5 7 9 10 8 6 4 2

Series Editors: Annie Hughes and Melanie Williams
Cinderella, Level 2, retold by Audrey McIlvain

Designed by Shireen Nathoo Design
Illustrated by Francesca Duffield

Printed in Scotland by Scotprint, Musselburgh

Published by Pearson Education Limited in association with Penguin Books Ltd,
both companies being subsidiaries of Pearson Plc

For a complete list of the title available in the Penguin Young Readers series please write to your local
Pearson education office or to: Marketing Department, Penguin Longman Publishing,
5 Bentinck Street, London W1M 5RN